ALEX AND THE WINTER STAR

Ann Coburn

ALEX AND THE WINTER STAR

OBERON BOOKS
LONDON

First published in 2009 by Oberon Books Ltd
521 Caledonian Road, London N7 9RH
Tel: 020 7607 3637 / Fax: 020 7607 3629
email: info@oberonbooks.com
www.oberonbooks.com

To find out more about Ann Coburn, go to www.anncoburn.com

To obtain Jim Kitson's original music for *Alex and the Winter
Star*, contact NTC (www.ntc-touringtheatre.co.uk) at Alnwick
Playhouse, Bondgate Without, Alnwick, Northumberland,
NE66 1PQ.

A catalogue record for this book is available from the British
Library.

Cover illustration by Helen Coburn

ISBN: 978-1-84002- 849-2

Acknowledgements

My thanks to:

Gillian Hambleton for making sure 'Forfun' stayed centre stage and for finding the magic once again.

Dominic Hughes, Janine Leigh, Lewis Matthews, Alan Park, Phil Yarrow and Sue Yarrow – a great team of actors who made *Alex and the Winter Star* shine!

Michelle Huitson for producing superb costumes and a versatile, imaginative set.

Ben Steppenbeck for lighting the way.

Jim Kitson for the wonderful music.

Anna Flood, Hilary Burns and Karen Hirst for putting the show on the road.

Ann Coburn

For my Alex

Characters

ALEX

CAT

SKARG 1

SKARG 2

THE WARRIOR

NEWSCASTER

HEAD TEACHER

(*Newscaster and Head Teacher can be played by the same actor.*)

UBIQUITOUS GRAVEL-VOICED AMERICAN (UGVA)
in voice-over only

Additional characters for schools or community performances:

STARWATCHERS

SHOPKEEPER

SHOPPER

CHILD WITH LOLLY

PARTY-GOERS

WINTER SPORTS PLAYERS

SCHOOL CHILDREN

ZOO ANIMALS

Alex and the Winter Star was first performed at Alnwick Playhouse by NTC Touring Theatre Company on 3 December 2005, with the following cast:

ALEX, Alan Park

WARRIOR, Phil Yarrow

CAT, Sue Yarrow

SKARG 1, Lewis Roberts

SKARG 2, Janine Leigh

HEAD TEACHER / NEWSCASTER, Dominic Hughes

All other parts played by members of the cast.

Directed by Gillian Hambleton

Assisted by Gavin Huscroft

Designed by Michelle Huitson

Assisted by Amanda Price

Music composed by Jim Kitson

Stage management and lighting by Ben Steppenbeck

Set built by Andy Ross

Costume maker Karen Holmes

For the NTC Touring Theatre Company:

General Manager Anna Flood

Tour Administrator Hilary Burns

Finance Co-ordinator Karen Hirst

Act One

SCENE ONE

ALEX, STARWATCHERS / SHOOTING STARS

The space should contain a number of stackable blocks of different sizes and shapes to be used as seats, desks, rocks, etc and to create different levels within the space. Throughout the play, the actors will move the blocks into the correct arrangement for each scene. In this scene – on top of Starwatcher's Hill – the blocks are rocks. A large frame at the back of the space would also be useful – as would a star curtain or glitter ball to create the impression of a star-filled sky when needed.

ALEX enters, wearing a scarf against the cold night. He is wearing a 'Starwatcher Club' badge and has a telescope or binoculars. He begins to search the sky. Other STARWATCHERS arrive, one by one (they can be played by other cast members if working with a small company). They also search the sky. A big meteor shower is expected. The STARWATCHERS start to sing as they study the sky.

ALL: Twinkle, twinkle little star…

Pause – search.

How I wonder where you are…

Pause – search.

Up above the sky so high –

Behind them, a shooting star zips across the sky with a whooshing noise (and perhaps a few notes of star music). They stop singing, whirl to look. The star has gone.

Like a diamond in the sky.
Twinkle, twinkle –

Whoosh! Another star shoots across the sky behind them. They whirl. Again they miss it.

Little star –

Whoosh!

How I wonder where you are…

A pause. They scan the sky. Then – whoosh, whoosh! Suddenly the sky is full of shooting stars. The star curtain/glitter ball should be used here. Star music plays. The STARWATCHERS all spin and point as they follow the path of the stars. It is as though STARWATCHERS and stars are dancing together. The star music dwindles, the shooting stars become less frequent and finally stop. The STARWATCHERS remain still for a beat staring up at the sky before they 'come back to earth'.

Twinkle, twinkle little star
How I wonder what you are.

The starwatchers move off.

ALEX: Bye then, Holly. See you at school.

HOLLY ignores him. ALEX watches her leave and then looks up at the sky.

Starlight, star bright,
Last star I see tonight.
I wish I may, I wish I might
Have the wish I wish tonight.

ALEX scans the sky. Nothing happens. He turns to walk away. One final shooting star whooshes across the sky.

(*To the star.*) Make Holly notice me!

ALEX exits.

SCENE TWO

CAT, NEWSCASTER, ALEX

ALEX's bedroom. A NEWSCASTER enters with a clipboard. NEWSCASTER is smartly dressed from the waist up but wearing pyjama bottoms. As CAT *(beautiful, haughty, white, with a noble pedigree) walks into* ALEX'S *room,* NEWSCASTER *signals off-screen. Frenetic news bulletin music plays. The* NEWSCASTER *raises his/her clipboard then realises his/her pyjama bottoms are on show.* NEWSCASTER *covers his/her embarrassment with clipboard and signals frantically off-screen. Frenetic news bulletin music stops.* NEWSCASTER *hurries behind desk and cues music again.* NEWSCASTER *proceeds to read the news, totally ignored by* CAT.

NEWSCASTER: Good Evening. Tonight's headlines once again.

Dong!

Ice to meet you! The big freeze comes to town.

Dong!

White out! Roads chaos in blizzard conditions.

Dong!

'Sno joke! Clear skies tonight but more of the white stuff heading our way.

NEWSCASTER *looks for some appreciation of her/his wordplay, but* CAT *is not listening. She is pacing the room.* NEWSCASTER *is put out at lack of response.*

And finally… Goodness, gracious, great balls of fire!

CAT *stops her pacing and turns to listen.* NEWSCASTER *looks pleased.*

The stars could be out in force tonight, but not on the red carpet. Who needs a red carpet when you have the whole sky? We're talking meteors. The Quadrantids, one of the biggest meteor showers of the year, are a winter highlight in our northern skies and many starwatchers are braving sub-zero temperatures tonight to catch the performance. But will it be a Christmas cracker or a frozen turkey? Just like some human superstars, the Quadrantids might not show up at all, leaving their disappointed fans standing in the cold. Still, as starwatchers always say, 'You may see a few, you may see many, but stay in your bed and you won't see any.'

NEWSCASTER winks/smiles.

CAT: Don't try to rhyme. It isn't smart.
We cats are masters of that art.

NEWSCASTER looks offended but recovers quickly.

NEWSCASTER: That's all from your late night news team.
We'll be back bright and early tomorrow. Good night
– and thanks for listening.

As the music marking the end of the bulletin begins to play, CAT harangues the NEWSCASTER.

CAT: Why would I listen to such rot?
Call that news? You should be shot!

Once again the human race
Fails to show a single trace

Of cleverness or common sense.
Compared with us you're all so dense.

We cats don't stand about for hours
Watching stupid meteor showers!

The NEWSCASTER makes a hasty exit. CAT moves to the window and looks out.

Come on Alex, hurry home.
You shouldn't leave me here alone.

You're my servant. Don't you see
That it's your job to worship me?

Serve food and drink, groom me for hours.
Not bunk off watching meteor showers!

I should've sacked you years ago.
One just can't find the staff you know.

ALEX enters, full of excitement. CAT is pleased to see him but trying not to show it. In all ensuing conversation, CAT understands ALEX perfectly but ALEX only hears purrs, miaows and yowls from CAT.

ALEX: There were hundreds of them! Hundreds!

ALEX does an impression of meteors whooshing across the sky.

CAT: Really? I'll have warm milk first
Just one bowl to quench my thirst.

ALEX: Clear sky too. We had no problems seeing them.

CAT: Fascinating. Salmon next.
Poached with herbs and lemon zest.

ALEX: We were up on the top of Starwatcher's Hill. And I stood right beside Holly.

CAT: How interesting. Now, for dessert –
Wait a minute! Red alert!

Holly is a female name.
Who is she and what's her game?

ALEX: I stood next to Holly and everything was sparkly.
The snow. The stars. Her eyes…

ALEX sighs and gazes into space. CAT reacts with horror.

CAT: I've heard of this disease before.
Furstluv, it's called. There is no cure.

ALEX checks his breath for freshness.

That Persian cat just down the road,
Her boy went into overload.

ALEX sniffs under his arms.

Took hours to gel and style his fur
And hardly gave a thought to her.

ALEX starts to arrange his hair. CAT gives a panicked whimper.

That cat looked like a right dog's dinner
Think Ozzy Osbourne, only thinner.

No snacks or games or daily groom –

ALEX smoothes down his clothes, checks for zits, practises his casual wave etc.

If Alex has Furstluv – I'm doomed!

ALEX: Eleven hours 'til I see Holly again at school.

CAT: Holly Schmolly!

ALEX: It's my turn to give a talk in assembly tomorrow. I'm going to talk about the stars! Maybe she'll notice me then. What do you think? Oh, no! I hope I don't get that – you know – nervous thing. If I get that – you know – nervous thing tomorrow... (*He groans.*) I need something to take my mind off it. What can I do...? I know! I'll play (*With mocking gravitas.*) 'The Warrior'. He's a bit past it these days, but I'll give him an outing, just for a laugh.

ALEX picks up his handset and begins to set up The Warrior computer game, but CAT won't leave him alone.

CAT: (*Imitating ALEX's mocking tone.*)
'The Warrior'. Aren't you mature?
You've grown up so much in a year.

If 'grown up' means you turn away
From friends you once saw every day.

ALEX: Stop yowling!

CAT: The Warrior came through for you
　　When you needed someone true.

　　He stepped right out of his own land
　　With courage high and sword in hand.

　　He saved the day – and learned to sing...
　　But you've forgotten everything.

ALEX: In a minute! I'm nearly done.

CAT: OK, I thought he was a wally
　　But frankly, rather him than Holly.

　　Am I the next friend you'll forget?
　　One last meal and then – the vet?

ALEX: There. That's loading. Now if I get you something to
　　eat, will you be quiet?

CAT: I'm not hungry, you big twit!
　　Well – maybe just a little bit...

ALEX: Come on then Snowball. Let's raid the kitchen.

ALEX exits followed by a grumbling CAT.

CAT: How many times? That's not my name.
　　Do listen while I try again.

　　My name is 'Queen Almighty
　　Sleekest Fur Alrighty
　　Sharpest Claws In Sighty
　　Prowling Gardens Nightly
　　Eyes a-shining brightly
　　Empress Aphrodite'.

　　I am a very noble cat –

CAT breaks off, sniffs.

　　Mmm, turkey – I'll have some of that.

CAT exits.

SCENE THREE

WARRIOR, SKARG 1, SKARG 2

The game finishes loading and the first, portentous notes of a Hollywood-blockbuster-type theme play as a PC game trailer/advert begins. The UBIQUITOUS GRAVEL-VOICED AMERICAN sets the scene in voice-over.

UGVA: A land – in peril. A people – in hiding. From the far reaches of space an evil beyond imagining has invaded their world.

Two SKARG enter, hooded and cloaked. Body movements obviously non-human, they make their malevolent way through the audience towards the central space.

The Skarg. Shapeshifting killers, their deadliest weapon is disguise. When evil can take any form, there is no safety. There is no escape. Only one man can save his people. Only one man can lead them. He is –

The music (along the lines of 'Eye of the Tiger') swells as WARRIOR enters, posing heroically before moving through the audience towards the central space. He is dressed something like a Gladiator. He carries a sword and a shield is strapped to his back. The whole scene is part trailer, part WWF opening event.

– The Warrior.

The Warrior. Never was a hero more needed
The Warrior. Available in all good stores now.
The Warrior. Are you tough enough?

The SKARG and WARRIOR engage in combat, showing off their fighting moves. This is a slick, impressive sequence with musical accompaniment.

Commencing actual game.

The three pause and then commence to demonstrate a sample of the actual game. This sequence is – frankly – pathetic, compared with the grand opening sequence. The music should show this. The fight ends with all three in a row at the back of the space, as though they are behind a monitor screen. They freeze in position. For a moment all is still but then the SKARG *begin a struggle to break out of the freeze-frame. The struggle is accompanied by music that builds tension and menace. There may be sparks and electrical crackles as their movements begin to rip through the fabric of the game. Soon they are able to move freely and the reason for their sudden ability to disobey the game rules becomes clear.* SKARG 1 *is carrying a patched-together Skarg-like version of* ALEX's *handset.* WARRIOR *remains frozen within the game.*

The SKARG *are still in their true form. Their movements are insectile, their 'speech' is a pattern of clicks, hisses etc.* SKARG 1 *retrieves a large egg-sac from its hiding place.* SKARG 2 *seems more interested in doing harm to a helpless* WARRIOR *but reluctantly turns back to the task in hand when* SKARG 1 *hisses an order. They brace themselves.* SKARG 1 *points the handset at the 'screen' and, with a final explosive accompaniment of sparks and crackles, they step through into* ALEX's *bedroom with the egg-sac. The* SKARG *share a celebratory moment – they have succeeded in breaking through the portal between their world and ours. They inspect* ALEX's *bedroom. They may even start sizing up the front rows of the audience, but when they hear* ALEX *returning, they flee, carrying their precious cargo between them.*

SCENE FOUR

ALEX, CAT, WARRIOR

ALEX *enters, followed by* CAT, *still licking her lips. While* CAT *settles down to a grooming session,* ALEX *picks up his handset and tries to play the game. The game music starts.* WARRIOR *draws his sword but there are no* SKARG *to tackle. The music fizzles out.* WARRIOR *gives an embarrassed shrug.*

ALEX: (*Throwing down the handset and turning his back on the screen.*) Broken! Stupid game! I wonder if Holly likes computer games?

ALEX goes into a dream about Holly. In the screen WARRIOR looks around, searching for the missing SKARG. He spots the cobbled-together handset, picks it up. His puzzlement turns to horror as he realises that the SKARG have worked out how to open a portal into ALEX's world. WARRIOR points the handset at the screen then drops it and moves forward, sword in hand. He tests the screen and then takes a deep breath and steps through into ALEX's bedroom. Instantly he goes into a crouch and begins to check every corner of the room. CAT leaps up and hurries over to ALEX.

CAT: Look out! Old leather-pants is back!
You knock him out. I'll find a sack.

ALEX: (*To himself, absent-mindedly patting CAT.*) I wonder if Holly has a pet?

WARRIOR has finished checking the room. Satisfied, he turns to look at ALEX and CAT. A broad grin spreads across his face.

CAT: Holly this and Holly that.
Why can't you understand plain cat?

We might just have a problem here.
The Warrior has reappeared.

ALEX: I wonder if Holly likes cats?

CAT: We'll shove him back into the game,
Then it's just me and you again.

WARRIOR: Greetings, Alex.

ALEX: Aaaaagggghhhh!

ALEX turns, sees WARRIOR, screams again. This stop-start sequence of screams continues – lessening in volume and length as WARRIOR *gradually identifies the boundaries of* ALEX's *'threat' zone.*

Aaaggghhh!

Hastily, WARRIOR *steps back.* ALEX *stops.* WARRIOR *steps forward again.*

Aaggghh!

WARRIOR *steps back.* ALEX *stops.* WARRIOR *puts out a hand.*

Aaa –

WARRIOR *withdraws hand – etc, etc. Finally,* ALEX *stops as* WARRIOR *steps back and stays there.* WARRIOR *raises his hands as though to say, 'I'm harmless', but the effect is spoiled when he nearly spears* CAT *with the large sword he is clutching.*

CAT: Do you mind? I like my skin.
It keeps germs out – and insides in.

WARRIOR *sheathes his sword.*

WARRIOR: Do not be afraid, creature. I know you are not meat. You belong to Alex. You are… (*A pause as he tries to recall the correct terminology.*) Apet.

CAT: Belong? A pet? I ought to sue!
You're really not worth talking to.

CAT *stalks off but continues to monitor the conversation.*

WARRIOR: Don't you remember me, Alex?

ALEX *hesitates, half shakes his head.*

I have never forgotten you.

ALEX *still looks unsure.*

ALEX: That's nice.

WARRIOR: Or our quest to rescue Mai'grand-ad.

ALEX: He's not your granddad. He's my granddad.

WARRIOR: That is what I said. Mai'grand-ad. It is a fine name.

ALEX: No, he's not your – oh, never mind.

WARRIOR: And is Mai'grand-ad well?

ALEX: Yes, he's doing fine, thanks.

WARRIOR: I kept the talisman.

ALEX: Good for you.

WARRIOR takes a small snow globe from the pouch on his belt.

WARRIOR: See?

ALEX: My snow globe! I thought I'd lost it.

WARRIOR: You gave me this talisman. Remember? Now, I return it to you.

WARRIOR shakes the globe and then holds it out. Warily, ALEX takes the snow globe. The solid object resting in his hand means he cannot deny that WARRIOR is standing in front of him.

ALEX: (*Shaking the globe.*) I thought that was all a dream. And now – are you real?

WARRIOR: (*Pointing to the globe, where the snow still swirls.*) I am as real as that snow.

ALEX: This isn't real snow.

WARRIOR: Not real?

ALEX: No – it's fake snow. But there's some real snow outside.

WARRIOR: There is? I would like to see that.

ALEX: Come to the window then.

ALEX beckons WARRIOR over. They stand side by side looking out at the snow. A little snow music plays.

WARRIOR: It is beautiful. So white and cold. Not like the hot, barren wastes of my world. They say it was different there once, before the Skarg came. The legends tell of a mild and pleasant land, with rich, dark soil and lakes full of fresh water. All gone now. All changed.

He looks sideways at ALEX.

You have changed too, my friend.

ALEX: Yeah, well. You know. Things move on…

WARRIOR: You have grown taller. And stronger, I think. Soon, you will make a fine young Warrior.

ALEX: Don't be daft! I mean, thanks. Thanks very much. But – I don't really want to be a Warrior.

WARRIOR: There is no choice, Alex. Every young man must become a warrior.

ALEX: In your world, maybe. But in my world there are loads of choices.

WARRIOR: There are?

ALEX: Yes. Some people choose to become soldiers – I mean warriors – but they don't have to. At least, not now. Not here.

WARRIOR: Hmm. There is much still to learn about your world. And much that I have forgotten, I fear. It is hard to think of anything but survival when every day is a battle against the Skarg. But I always remembered you, my friend. Just as I promised.

ALEX: Yes. You said.

WARRIOR: So, if you are not to be a Warrior, what will you choose to do?

ALEX: When I was little I wanted to drive an ice cream van – or a bus!

WARRIOR: And now?

ALEX: My mum wants me to be something boring and safe. But I want to be an astronomer.

WARRIOR: What is an ass – asstro – what is that? Is it like a commander?

ALEX: No. An astronomer studies the stars.

WARRIOR: What are stars? Are they a kind of weapon?

ALEX: No.

WARRIOR: A defensive trick then –

ALEX: No! Look, why have you come back? I don't mean to be rude, but I don't need your help this time. And I didn't make a wish. At least, I didn't wish for, you know…

ALEX makes a gesture to encompass his room with WARRIOR standing in the middle of it.

WARRIOR: For me?

ALEX: No.

WARRIOR: Oh. Then what did you wish for, Alex?

ALEX: Nothing. Well, nothing much. Except, there's this girl. Holly.

CAT: Holly, schmolly.

ALEX: I like her. But she doesn't even know I exist. So tonight I wished on a star. I wished for her to notice me.

WARRIOR looks increasingly puzzled.

WARRIOR: Why do you like this Holly person?

ALEX: She's, you know, a girl.

WARRIOR: But why do you like this Agirl?

ALEX: (*Highly embarrassed.*) Shut up!

WARRIOR: Is this Agirl a good warrior?

ALEX: No.

WARRIOR: A great hunter?

ALEX: No.

WARRIOR: Then I am puzzled, Alex. Why do you like her?

ALEX: Because – shut up!

WARRIOR: Hmmm. No matter. It is not your wishing that brings me to this world a second time. It is the Skarg.

A harsh sigh fills the space. CAT and ALEX both look terrified. CAT forgets about being haughty and hurries over to be close to ALEX. They both look at the blank screen, around the room and back to WARRIOR.

ALEX: Skarg?

WARRIOR: (*In game mode, as though he is briefing new resistance fighters.*) Skarg are giant insects with razor sharp teeth and claws that carry a deadly poison. They are shape-shifters, able to change their appearance at will. A Skarg could be standing among us right now, but only an expert like me would be able to tell. These vicious invaders move from world to world like a plague, taking what they need and destroying the rest. They show no mercy –

CAT: (*Still glancing nervously from side to side.*)
Nor do you! Don't drone on so!
Just tell us what we need to know!

WARRIOR: Alex, you must keep your Apet quiet. The Skarg could be close by –

ALEX: Close? What do you mean? There are no Skarg in this world. Are there?

WARRIOR: No! None!

Except for two.

ALEX / CAT: What!

WARRIOR: Alex, the Skarg are fiendishly clever and incredibly greedy. I should have known that once they discovered this earth of yours they would try to return.

Pointing to the screen.

They invented a device to reopen the portal between our worlds. Then, when you began the – Loading Ceremony – just now, they came through. They are here somewhere. Two of them. They have come for their revenge against the one who stopped their evil plans last time.

Pointing to ALEX.

That's you.

ALEX: It is? Well, can't somebody just tell them it wasn't me?

WARRIOR: No need. For I have returned!

Both CAT and ALEX look distinctly underwhelmed. WARRIOR tries again.

For I have returned!

To protect you. Against the Skarg.

ALEX: How are you planning to do that?

WARRIOR: (*In hero mode.*) I shall stay by your side, night and day. I won't leave you for a second –

ALEX: You can't do that!

WARRIOR: I know. It will be a hard task, but I shall meet the challenge –

ALEX: No! I mean, I have to go to school and stuff.

WARRIOR: Then I shall go to the skoolanstuf too. What is a skoolanstuf?

ALEX: No. You can't come to school. I can't let Holly see you with me – I mean, you don't need to protect me at school. It's perfectly safe. Besides, if any Skarg had stepped through into my bedroom, I think I would have noticed. I bet they're hiding somewhere back in your world. You should go. I'll be fine!

ALEX tries to push WARRIOR back into the screen. WARRIOR does not budge.

WARRIOR: No, Alex. I shall not leave your side.

ALEX: Well, that's just great!

ALEX storms off. WARRIOR remains for a moment, looking puzzled and a bit hurt and lost.

WARRIOR: I do not understand. Why does Alex walk away from me?

CAT: Don't be upset. You're not to blame.
He's caught furstluv. It's such a shame.

He thinks you're going to cramp his style
He thinks you'll make her run a mile.

I have to say I think he's right.
You might be useful in a fight

But Holly won't be too impressed
With your dirty leather vest.

So I think you should carry on
'Til Holly's well and truly gone.

WARRIOR: I think you are trying to communicate with me
creature, but I have no knowledge of your yowling
language.

He yowls and miaows experimentally. CAT rolls her eyes.

No matter. The Warrior shall not fail a friend, even
when the friend is unwilling to accept his help. Come,
creature! We must stay close to Alex!

WARRIOR draws his sword and hurries off.

CAT: Alex, your wish has just come true.
Holly will soon notice you!

She may ignore you as a rule
But if you turn up at the school

With him in leather underwear,
You're guaranteed to get a stare.

*CAT smirks but then realises that she has been left on her own.
She looks around, suddenly afraid. Another harsh Skarg-sigh
sends her hurrying after ALEX and WARRIOR.*

SCENE FIVE

SKARG 1, SKARG 2

*The space becomes a dark cave. SKARG 1 and 2 enter carrying the egg
sac. They are still in insect form. They lower the egg sac to the ground
before checking out the cave. Once they are satisfied that there is no
lurking danger, the SKARG begin to change into human form. They
straighten up and squirm to get comfortable inside their new skin,
trying to sort out the shape-shifters equivalent of a 'wedgie'.*

SKARG 1: Once again we must suffer the discomfort of being
hu-man.

SKARG 2: Such a tight fit. And such ugly bodies. But their soft flesh will make good eating.

SKARG 2 licks her lips hungrily.

SKARG 1: Patience, Private Nee – sta – ch – ch – pik. First there is work to do.

SKARG 2: Yes sir!

They both turn to the egg sac.

SKARG 1: (*Fondly.*) Look at the little beauties squirming around in there! Two hundred Skarg maggots, all of them queens. Once they change into fully grown Skarg and start laying eggs of their own, this planet – this earth – will fall under our control.

To the maggots, in a baby-talk voice, much to SKARG 2's discomfort

Won't it? Won't the nasty old earth fall under our controlly-wolly?

SKARG 2: Sir?

SKARG 1: Oh yes it will! Oh yes it will!

SKARG 2: Sir!

SKARG 1 straightens up and gets himself under control.

SKARG 1: Yes. As I was saying. The maggots will be safe here.

SKARG 2: And look! (*Pointing to the frame.*) There is the perfect nursery!

SKARG 1: Really? I mean, I knew that. Why else would I lead us here? (*Inspecting the space behind the frame.*) Good. As I thought. It is a deep hole – dark and dry, with none of that nasty, cold white stuff. That – what is it called, Private?

The SKARG proceed to lift the egg sac into the frame and lower it into the hole out of sight

SKARG 2: Snow.

SKARG 1: Schhno-o-o-ww…

They both shudder.

That will have to go. Soon this earth will become like all our other conquests.

SKARG 2: Sir?

SKARG 1: Hot, dry and dusty.

SKARG 2: Sir?

SKARG 1: A perfect Skarg environment!

SKARG 2: Sir! Our maggots must be fed soon if they are to survive.

SKARG 1: I was just coming to that! Access your data banks, Private. Find out the hu-man name for the food we need.

SKARG 2: (*Plugs finger in ear or similar and begins an information search.*) Oh! Oh no! It can't be.

SKARG 1: What is the problem? Tell me!

SKARG 2: Brad and Jen have split up! [*Or equivalent topical showbiz news.*] When did that happen?

SKARG 1: Brad and – ? You're doing it again, aren't you? You're tuning in to – 'Sky Movies'.

SKARG 2: I'm so out of date. Brad's with Angelina now – Oh! You'll never guess what they're doing on Big Brother –

SKARG 1 shakes SKARG 2

SKARG 1: I – don't – care!

He lets SKARG 2 *go and turns his back.*

SKARG 2: 'Shaken. Not stirred.'

SKARG 1: Private!

SKARG 2: Sugar.

SKARG 1: What did you call me?

SKARG 2: Sugar. That is the hu-man name for the food we must collect.

SKARG 1: Shoogar. Good. Now, how to find it? Shoogar... Shoogar...

SKARG 1 paces back and forth, the picture of concentration. Behind him, SKARG 2 produces a home-made detecting device (could be something like a tommy-gun).

SKARG 2: Sir?

SKARG 1: Be quiet! I'm trying to think.

SKARG 2: (*Waving the device.*) But, sir –

SKARG 1: Will you stop waving that thing around! What is it, anyway?

SKARG 2: A shoogar – I mean sugar – detector.

SKARG 1: Where did that come from?

SKARG 2: I made it, sir, in preparation for our invasion.

SKARG 1: Does it work?

Enthusiastically, SKARG 2 switches on the sugar detector, raises it to her shoulder and prepares to demonstrate.

SKARG 2: Of course! If there is sugar nearby, the detector will point us towards it, like this –

The detector swings around violently, taking SKARG 2 with it and knocking SKARG 1 sideways. SKARG 2, unaware that she has just floored SKARG 1, comes to a halt with the detector pointing off-stage. The detector is quivering with energy and SKARG 2 can hardly hold it back.

Oh, sir! There is so much sugar in this area!

SKARG 2 turns off the detector and turns to SKARG 1 who by this time has recovered.

But it is all in the hu-man settlement.

SKARG 1: Then let us go and take the shoogar from these puny earthlings!

SKARG 1 begins to exit, changing into his true form as he goes.

SKARG 2: Stop!

SKARG 1 pauses.

Sir… I am sure what you meant to say was, we cannot reveal our true form to these earthlings until all our maggots are fully grown.

SKARG 1: I did? Why would I say that?

SKARG 2: Well Sir, you were wise enough to know that two Skarg racing into town and ripping people's heads off might cause a bit of a stir.

SKARG 1: It would…? Yes, it would!

SKARG 2: And then the hu-mans would bring their army to this place and kill our maggots.

SKARG 1 screams / gasps in horror.

Of course, once we have our Skarg army, nothing can stop us.

SKARG 1: Aha! Then we shall reveal our true form!

SKARG 2: But for now…

SKARG 2 nods at SKARG 1 in an expectant sort of way. SKARG 1 remains blank. SKARG 2 gives up and continues.

For now, we must collect the sugar in our hu-man disguise.

SKARG 1: Oh. (*Shrugging uncomfortably back into full human form.*) That's a disappointment.

SKARG 2: No matter, sir. We are much better prepared to be hu-man this time. For instance, I have been researching hu-man names.

SKARG 1: Not like last time, then? That was your idea, wasn't it, Private? To take our names from the first things we saw?

SKARG 2: Sir?

SKARG 1: Remind me. What name did you choose?

SKARG 2: (*Unwillingly.*) Bus Stop.

SKARG 1 laughs.

And you, sir? What name did you choose?

SKARG 1 stops laughing.

SKARG 1: I don't recall.

SKARG 2: Taxi Rank, wasn't it? Although you rather fancied Dorothy Perkins –

SKARG 1: Enough of that! What have you learned about hu-man names?

SKARG 2: I consulted a research document known as Hello Magazine.

SKARG 1: And?

SKARG 2: Many Hollywood stars name their hatchlings after earth towns or cities, such as Chelsea or Dakota. Brooklyn or Preston.

SKARG 1: Preston?

SKARG 2: I thought, sir, you might want to name yourself after the place where our invasion began.

SKARG 1: Yes… Yes I like that idea. What is the name of this place?

SKARG 2: Alnwick. [*Or insert the name of the place where the play is being performed.*]

They look at one another doubtfully and then shake their heads.

SKARG 1 / 2: No.

SKARG 2: Many hu-man celebrities name themselves after a strong, bold animal. Tiger Woods. Richard the Lionheart –

SKARG 1: Yes! You may have something there, Private. I shall choose a name from the insect kingdom, in honour of our race. Now let me think… A merciless invader, sweeping through the land, feeding on the blood of its hu-man victims… I know! I shall be – a nit!

SKARG 2: (*Accessing data banks.*) The headlouse, more commonly known as a nit. Good choice, sir! You are a nit!

SKARG 1: Thank you, Private. Now you.

SKARG 2: Well, Sir. According to Hello Magazine it is fashionable for celebs to name their hatchlings after fruit, such as Peaches, or Apple. So, I thought I could be – Bananas!

SKARG 1: Very well, Private. You're Bananas and I'm a Nit. Now, let us go and find some sugar.

They exit, with SKARG 2 still clutching the sugar detector.

SCENE SIX

SCHOOL CHILDREN, ALEX, CAT, WARRIOR,
HEAD TEACHER, SKARG 1, SKARG 2

Snow music starts. ALEX, CAT and WARRIOR enter (with a crowd of school children if cast size permits), throwing snowballs, skidding on the ice etc. The HEAD TEACHER summons them all inside. As everyone troops off into the school, SKARG 1 and 2 enter. SKARG 2 is operating the detector. Suddenly it swings violently towards the exiting children. SKARG 1 is ready for this. He ducks and the detector swings over his head. He straightens with a smug smile, but the detector swings round full circle and whacks him on the back of the head.

SKARG 2: (*Unaware.*) Oh, Nit! There is a great deal of sugar in this building.

SKARG 1: (*Grabbing the sugar detector.*) Give me that!

Throughout the ensuing conversation SKARG 1 is attempting to figure out how to use the detector.

SKARG 2: As you wish, Nit. If you look at the monitor reading, you will see that most of the sugar here is in the form of something called a sweetie.

SKARG 1: Sweetie?

SKARG 2: Yes darling? I mean, yes, Nit. Sweeties. Ah! Here is one!

SKARG 2 bends to pick up a dropped sweet just as SKARG 1 gets the detector working. It swings towards the school, passing harmlessly over SKARG 2's head. SKARG 1, taken by surprise by the force of the swing, once again ends up on his back/knees/off-balance.

SKARG 2 straightens, studying the sweet.

Human maggots seem to like them a lot.

SKARG 1: (*Scrambling to his feet.*) Too bad! They can't have them!

SKARG 1 begins to march towards the school.

SKARG 2: Wait a minute, Nit!

SKARG 1: What is it now, Bananas?

SKARG 2: This building has high security. We cannot simply walk in.

SKARG 1: (*Making a hasty retreat and regarding the school warily.*) Hmmm. The hu-mans must value this sugar very highly. What is this place? An army base?

SKARG 2: (*Accessing data banks.*) No. It is – (*Pause – SKARG 1 waits nervously.*) Aha!

SKARG 1 jumps at the sudden noise and then glares at SKARG 2.

SKARG 1: What?

SKARG 2: It is a school. A place where human maggots are trained. (*Another pause.*) Aha!

SKARG 1: (*Jumping again.*) What!

SKARG 2: There is a way to get into this school and take the sweeties without any resistance.

SKARG 1: How?

SKARG 2 does a loud and sudden imitation of a dentist's drill. SKARG 1 jumps again. SKARG 2 steps up and whispers in SKARG 1's ear.

Aha!

Both SKARG *do an imitation of a dentist's drill. They share a wicked laugh and exit to the accompaniment of 'dastardly deed' type music.*

SCENE SEVEN

ALEX, CAT, WARRIOR, HEAD TEACHER, PUPILS
(if cast size allows – or SKARG 1 and 2 can make up the numbers)

Everyone files on stage and takes up position. The HEAD TEACHER *taps a baton and begins to conduct. They sing a beautiful carol ('Silent Night' or 'It Came Upon a Midnight Clear' or similar).*

WARRIOR: Good! Let us sing again! Sing! Sing!

ALEX: Be quiet!

WARRIOR: But Alex, I remember now. The singing is wonderful –

ALEX: Shhh!

The pupils sit around the edge of the space. ALEX *is looking extremely nervous. The* HEAD TEACHER *addresses the audience as though they were the assembled school. Although the speech consists mostly of blah blahs, the meaning should be clear from tone of voice etc.*

HEAD TEACHER: Lovely singing but stand like tall trees and fill your lungs!

Now, a few notices.

Blah, blah, blah – bronze medal in the cross-country!

Applauds, frowning at any audience member who does not join in. ALEX, CAT *and* WARRIOR *hastily join the applause.*

Blah blah blah – wads of wet tissue paper on the ceiling.

Frowns/glares at audience.

Blah, blah, blah – volunteers to pick up litter?

Pauses, smiles expectantly at audience. Smile disappears, replaced by scowl.

Blah, Blah, blah – meet me in the playground at breaktime. Bring your own black sacks.

Interrupted by ringtone – steps forward. Glares at audience until ringtone stops.

Blah blah blah – will be confiscated!

Blah blah blah – no snowballs in the corridor!

Blah blah blah – ice slides in the teachers' car park are not funny!

Another glare, rubbing sore bottom at same time.

And finally, continuing our tradition of talks in assembly, this morning we have Alex and his – um – (*HEAD TEACHER gives WARRIOR and CAT the once over. They return the compliment.*) – assistants – to tell us all about the stars.

HEAD TEACHER leads audience in applause, glaring at those who do not immediately join in. The stage belongs to ALEX.

SCENE EIGHT

ALEX, CAT, WARRIOR, HEAD TEACHER,
CONSTELLATIONS (worked by cast members)

ALEX steps forward, clearly terrified. He is clutching a sheet of paper. Throughout the first part of his talk, ALEX is afflicted with hiccups.

ALEX: There are ten – (*Hiccups.*) –

WARRIOR and CAT look at ALEX in astonishment.

Um – 'scuse me. I'll start again. (*Referring to paper he takes a deep breath.*) There are ten thousand billion billion stars in our universe…

ALEX gives a sigh of relief followed by a big hiccups. If young audience members are laughing at this stage, WARRIOR draws his sword and steps forward threateningly. CAT also steps forward and glares. ALEX waves them back.

(Hiccups.) Sorry. Um. *(To himself, finding his place on the paper.)* Ten thousand billion billion… Oh, yes. A-and these stars are divided up into thousands of galaxies – *(Hiccups.)*

Our galaxy is called The Milk – *(Hiccups.)* – y Way – *(Hiccups.)*

Again WARRIOR and CAT step forward. ALEX waves them back.

It has – um – lots of constellations – *(Hiccups x 3.)* –

WARRIOR and CAT step forward. This time WARRIOR looks like he means business. In desperation, ALEX abandons his prepared speech. Instead he really begins to talk to the audience.

Forget about numbers. Stars are brilliant! If you're lost, the stars will show you the way home. In fact, once you know which stars to look for, you can find your way to anywhere on earth! And the stars are easy to find, because they make shapes in the sky. It's like join the dots. People join up the dots and they say, 'Oh! That looks like a scorpion! Or, 'I can see a wolf!' If you go out tonight and look up, you might see a lion with a big mane.

The first Chinese-style paper (or cloth) and rod puppet appears. A brightly coloured lion, with the Leo constellation marked out on his body in bright stars. Leo swoops and dances around the space as Alex talks. Star music begins to build.

He's called Leo. There's a beautiful swan, too.

Cygnus the swan appears.

She's called Cygnus. There are all sorts of animals in the night sky. There's a fox, and a bear. And a fierce, charging bull, called Taurus.

Taurus appears.

But my favourite constellation of all is Draco, the dragon!

Draco appears. The constellation puppets continue to dance and swoop around the space as ALEX concludes his talk.

And did you know the stars can sing?

The STAR PUPPET WRANGLERS begin to sing, a simple one word song, a pulsing that weaves into the star music.

STAR WRANGLERS: Shine…shine…shine.

ALEX: They send out sound waves. Like a pulse. Like a beat.

The song builds into a harmony, growing in complexity and creating a rhythm.

But sound won't travel through space so we've never been able to hear them.

A silent pause.

Until now.

Music/song continues.

Now there's a special telescope that can pick up the sound waves for us to hear.

And we should listen. Because the stars are part of us. We are made of stardust. Imagine that! Just about every bit of us, carbon, oxygen, nitrogen, was made inside a star more than five billion years ago. The star exploded and scattered stardust all across the universe – and some of it landed here. Stars R Us. We are stars. We all belong here in our universe. We all belong together.

Stars are brilliant! And they're always there. All you need to do is notice them. The next time you step out into the dark, look up. You'll be amazed.

SCENE NINE

ALEX, CAT, WARRIOR, SKARG 1, SKARG 2, HEAD TEACHER

HEAD TEACHER leads the audience in applause for ALEX. ALEX, CAT and WARRIOR move to the side of the space. ALEX is hugely relieved. He is thinking this day might not be such a disaster after all. He doesn't know what's coming next.

HEAD TEACHER: Thank you Alex. I'm sure we all enjoyed that. And now we have an extra, surprise talk. Two very important dentists have come to see us today. They're going to tell us how to care for our teeth.

SKARG 1 and SKARG 2 sidle onto the stage. They are wearing white coats and may be wearing other 'dentist' props in bizarre ways. SKARG 1 has the sugar detector.

Would you like to introduce yourselves to the children?

SKARG 1: Of course, Head Case.

SKARG 2: (*Hissing.*) Head Teacher!

SKARG 1: I mean Head Creature. I'm a nit – and she's bananas.

SKARG 2: Let's start with – Sweeties! Sweeties are very, very bad! Sweeties kill your teeth!

SKARG 1 begins scanning the audience with the detector.

SKARG 1: Yep. Poor, poor little toothie pegs. Bad sweeties kill 'em stone dead. And you know what happens then, don't you, maggots? I mean children?

The SKARG both do an imitation of a dentist's drill.

SKARG 2: So, hand them over. All the sweeties. Bad, bad sweeties! Give them to us. Now!

SKARG 1: Right now! All the sweeties! Hand them over! Come on!

WARRIOR has been looking at the sugar detector with growing suspicion. Now he gets to his feet. SKARG 1 and 2 see him for the first time. They gasp. They freeze in place. The WARRIOR is the last person they expected to see in this world. He is a real threat to their invasion plans.

WARRIOR: (*Pointing to the sugar detector.*) Let me see that device.

Hastily, SKARG 1 hides the detector behind his back.

SKARG 1: What device?

WARRIOR: It looks like Skarg technology to me!

He tries to step forward, but ALEX grabs his arm. CAT sits back, enjoying the way the situation is developing.

ALEX: (*Whispering.*) Please don't do this to me! Holly's just over there!

WARRIOR: But they may be Skarg, Alex.

HEAD TEACHER: Sit down please!

To the SKARG as ALEX drags a reluctant WARRIOR back to his seat.

Do continue.

The SKARG are at a loss for words. SKARG 1 does not dare to bring the sugar detector into view again. SKARG 2 has an idea. She hurries to stand behind SKARG 1, pushing her arms through so that they look like his arms. SKARG 1 continues to stand with his own arms behind his back, hiding the sugar detector.

SKARG 2: Talk!

SKARG 1: What?

SKARG 2: Talk! About teeth!

SKARG 1: Listen carefully, maggots. This is how to clean your teeth.

Throughout the following speech, SKARG 1 has to improvise as SKARG 2's hands do various things to his face. For example…

First, open wide.

SKARG 2 hooks fingers in his mouth and pulls it open. SKARG 1 shakes his head to dislodge them.

But not as wide as that. Then you…check your nose, to make sure no teeth are hiding up there. If they are, you… Slap! Your face. Then you… Slap! Your face again. That should get them out. Then you take your toothbrush –

SKARG 2 extends a rigid finger. SKARG 1 looks at it apprehensively.

And you… Poke yourself in the face a few times. Then you use the toothbrush to – comb your hair. Now, with both hands you… Squeeze your cheeks together so that you look like a duck. Then you… Cover up your eyes so you can't see a thing, pull out your ears and do a monkey impression. Then you do a hand jive and, to finish off… You get some water and then… throw it over your shoulder! Again… over the other shoulder! Then you pat – I SAID PAT! – your face dry.

HEAD TEACHER: Thank you, Nit and Bananas. I think we've heard enough. And now, a final carol to end the assembly.

HEAD TEACHER produces baton again and clears throat. With SKARG 1 and 2 standing one side of him and ALEX, CAT and a very suspicious WARRIOR standing the other, HEAD TEACHER taps the baton and they sing a lively carol ('I Saw Three Ships' or similar) as they march out of assembly and exit. HEAD TEACHER hustles ALEX, CAT and a reluctant WARRIOR in front of him/her one way, while SKARG 1 and 2 march off the other way.

SKARG 1 / 2: We'll be back!

End of Act One.

Act Two

OPENING NUGGET

SKARG 1, SKARG 2

The SKARG *are prowling the space as the audience return from the interval.* SKARG 2 *has the sugar detector and is checking for sweets.* SKARG 1 *homes in on every rustling sweet wrapper, asking for sweets. Once the audience is settled, the scene begins.*

SCENE ONE

SKARG 1, SKARG 2, SHOPKEEPER, SHOPPER, CHILD

SKARG 1: These maggots guard their sweeties far too well. We must look for sugar elsewhere.

SKARG 2: But not in schools. The Warrior may be searching for us there.

SKARG 1: The Warrior! How dare he follow us through into this world! No matter – he will die soon, alongside his puny earth friends.

SKARG 2: Nit? Apologies, but if we don't find sugar soon, the only things dying will be our maggots.

SKARG 1: Ah, yes. The sugar. (*Standing well back.*) Scan the area, Bananas.

SKARG 2: I'm on to it, Nit.

SKARG 2 scans the area. The detector swings towards a supermarket sign.

[NB *If you are working with a small cast, at this point it is possible to cut to the end of the scene, when the* SKARG *attempt to steal the sugar from the shop. This does away with the* SHOPKEEPER, SHOPPER *and* CHILD.]

A SHOPKEEPER appears in the frame at the back of the space.

SKARG 2: Aha! Pure sugar! Bags and bags of it! Our maggots will eat well tonight.

SKARG 1: Oh really? And how do we take the sugar away from the human? Just walk right up and ask him for some?

A SHOPPER enters and walks up to the SHOPKEEPER.

SHOPPER: Bag of sugar please.

SHOPKEEPER: Certainly.

SKARG 1 watch in astonishment as the SHOPPER goes off with a bag of sugar.

SKARG 1 pushes SKARG 2 towards the SHOPKEEPER.

SKARG 2: Sugar.

SHOPKEEPER: Certainly. How much would you like?

SKARG 2: (*Giving SKARG 1 a delighted look.*) All of it.

SHOPKEEPER: All two hundred bags?

SKARG 2: (*Holding out hand.*) Yes.

SHOPKEEPER: That'll be three hundred pounds please.

SKARG 2 withdraws hand and looks questioningly at SKARG 1. SKARG 1 shrugs.

SKARG 2: (*Holding out hand.*) Yes.

SHOPKEEPER: First you have to give me the money.

SKARG 2: Money?

SHOPKEEPER: Money. Dosh. Readies. Cash. Bread. Brass. Lolly. Give it to me.

Pause. SKARG 2 withdraws hand and hurries over to SKARG 1.

SKARG 1: What's the problem?

SKARG 2: He says we have to give him a lolly first.

SKARG 1 and 2 again check out the front rows of the audience. A child enters and skips across the space, singing happily. He/she is holding a lolly.

SKARG 1: (*To SKARG 2.*) Where are you going?

SKARG 2: I'm going to make her an offer she can't refuse.

SKARG 2 hijacks the lolly. CHILD does an Oscar-winning dejected walk-off. SKARG 2 takes the lolly to the SHOPKEEPER, who has seen the whole hijack.

SHOPKEEPER: Who do you think you are?

SKARG 2: I'm Bananas and he's a Nit.

SHOPKEEPER: You can say that again!

SHOPKEEPER turns his sign to 'CLOSED' and exits.

SKARG 1: Ooohhh! He will have to go! Pesky humans. I can't wait to destroy them. Give me that!

He snatches the lolly from SKARG 2 just as she is about to take a lick.

This will not feed our maggots. How can we get more sugar?

SKARG 2 points towards the empty shop.

SKARG 2: We could steal it.

The SKARG share a look of delight before changing into their insect form. The lights go down. There follows a scene straight out of a silent movie. The SKARG search the aisles, bumping into shelves and backing into one another. Every time they make a noise, a spotlight picks them out. They freeze. The spotlight clicks off – and so on until they find a sack of sugar and make off with it.

SCENE TWO

ALEX, CAT, WARRIOR

ALEX, CAT and WARRIOR enter. They have climbed to the top of Starwatcher's Hill.

ALEX: Don't look up yet.

WARRIOR obeys. ALEX leads him into the centre of the space, climbing over the blocks. An exhausted CAT follows.

CAT: Did we have to climb so high?
Just to stare up at the sky?

WARRIOR: Now?

ALEX: (*Beckoning WARRIOR onwards.*) Not yet.

CAT: (*Staggering theatrically.*)
I'm feeling faint. The air's so thin…
I think I must need oxygen…

Checks to see whether her performance has had any effect, but is irritated to discover that ALEX and WARRIOR are both ignoring her.

Call mountain rescue! I could do
With Kendal Mint Cake and a brew.

Again, CAT is ignored. She goes into a sulk.

ALEX: Ok. Now you can look up.

WARRIOR looks up and sees the stars. He is amazed. Maybe star music and lighting here?

What do you think?

WARRIOR: So many. And so bright.

ALEX: Yeah. That's why I brought you to the top of
Starwatcher's Hill. Down there, with all the street lights
and stuff, it's hard to see the stars. But up here…

WARRIOR: I have never seen anything like it.

ALEX: Are there no stars in your world?

WARRIOR: (*Shaking his head.*) Only five red moons.

ALEX: (*Handing WARRIOR binoculars or telescope.*) Here. Take a closer look.

WARRIOR looks through the binoculars at the audience. He jumps backwards with a horrified look on his face, then glares suspiciously between the binoculars and the audience.

Point them upwards.

WARRIOR follows instructions and once again is amazed. CAT is becoming interested despite herself and sidles up to stand beside them. Still complaining, she gazes up at the stars too.

CAT: Can we please get off this hill
Before I catch a nasty chill?

If this is what you do with Holly,
You really must be off your trolley...

ALEX pats CAT. Her complaints die away. WARRIOR hands the binoculars back to ALEX, who strings them around his neck. CAT leans against ALEX.

A pause while they all look up at the stars.

ALEX: (*Pointing.*) Pollux!

CAT and WARRIOR both turn to stare at ALEX then they both give the audience a worried glance.

CAT / WARRIOR: Pardon?

ALEX: Pollux. That star there, see? He's called Pollux.

CAT / WARRIOR: (*Relieved.*) Oh...

ALEX: And there's his brother, Castor. They're the Gemini twins.

WARRIOR: Is there a warrior up there?

ALEX: Um… There's a charioteer.

WARRIOR: (*Striking a pose.*) Aha!

ALEX: He's called Auriga. And look, there's Orion. He's a hunter, with a sword and a shield and a star-studded belt.

WARRIOR: (*Striking another pose.*) Is he a good hunter?

ALEX: I expect so. He wouldn't be up there otherwise. It's an honour you see.

WARRIOR: An honour?

ALEX: Yes. There are stories about them. How they were so brave, the gods honoured them by turning them into stars, so they would be remembered.

WARRIOR: For how long?

ALEX: Pretty much for ever. The stars are always there. People thousands of years ago were looking at the same stars we can see tonight.

WARRIOR: And thousands of years hence?

CAT: Hence? What sort of word is that? Speak English – or you could try Cat.

ALEX: You mean in the future? Yes. I'm sure people will still be looking at the stars. And writing songs about them.

WARRIOR: Songs! That is indeed an honour. And you, Alex. Why do you like stars so much?

ALEX: Well, they sort of make me feel safe. I used to be scared of the dark –

WARRIOR: I remember. You no longer had your kinsman
Mai'dad to watch over you. The darkness made you feel
lonely and lost.

ALEX: Yes. But now I never feel alone in the dark.

WARRIOR: Because the stars watch over you?

ALEX: Yeah. And I know I won't get lost either. The stars
will always show me the way.

WARRIOR: Both a guardian and a guide. That is a noble
thing to be.

A pause. They gaze up at the stars.

An honour…

*Suddenly ALEX turns to CAT, who is also caught up in the
mood of entrancement.*

ALEX: Look Snowball! That's Sirius. The dog star.

CAT: Dog? Did you say Dog? Dog where?
Is it hiding over there?

Is it creeping up on me?
I need a fence, a wall, a tree!

WARRIOR: Why is your Apet yowling?

ALEX: I think she must have heard the word 'dog'. (*To CAT,
speaking with exaggerated slowness.*) It's all right Snowball.
I said 'dog star'. Star. Up there. That's Sirius. He's
Orion's hunting dog and he's the brightest single star in
the whole sky.

CAT: The brightest star? I don't think so!
Dogs are dull and thick and slow.

And tell me, just who was the nut
Who named a star after a mutt!

CAT stalks off.

ALEX: (*To WARRIOR.*) See that house at the bottom of the hill? Holly lives there.

CAT: Holly, schmolly!

WARRIOR: Ah. Holly. The Agirl at the skoolanstuff.

ALEX: Yes, the one who was sitting right in the front row when you went for those two dentists.

WARRIOR: I thought they were Skarg!

ALEX: You thought the school caretaker was a Skarg too. I've never seen him run so fast. And what about my Geography teacher? It took me ages to get that waste paper bin off her head. I thought you were supposed to be an expert at spotting Skarg?

WARRIOR: She looked like a Skarg in disguise. Did you see how she kept twitching?

ALEX: She's a teacher! They all twitch!

WARRIOR: And she kept snarling the same word over and over again. 'Sats! Sats!'

ALEX: I'm telling you, she's human!

WARRIOR: But the dentists, Alex. I am sure they were not human.

ALEX: No. They were dentists.

WARRIOR: I do not understand. Are dentists a different species?

ALEX: Never mind. You're right. They were a bit odd. But they can't be Skarg.

WARRIOR: Why not?

ALEX: Because you said the Skarg had come back to get me, but those two dentists weren't interested in me at all.

WARRIOR: Ah, but they were fearful when they caught sight of me.

ALEX: So was the caretaker. And my Geography teacher.

WARRIOR: But –

ALEX: Look. If you start waving a dirty great sword around people – even dentists – will be scared. There's no New Game here, remember?

WARRIOR: I remember. Those who die in this world do not return. Game over. Like your kinsman, Mai'dad.

ALEX: Yes. Like my dad... Anyway, if they had really been Skarg, Snowball would have sniffed them out right away. Wouldn't you Snowball?

CAT: (*To WARRIOR.*) Normally I would have done
But I was having too much fun

Watching Alex groan and blush
as his love life turned to dust.

ALEX: Admit it. I'm right, aren't I? There are no Skarg here. You embarrassed me in front of Holly for nothing.

WARRIOR: I am sorry, Alex. I will make it up to you. I will bring the Agirl Holly to this place right now.

WARRIOR sets off towards Holly's house.

ALEX: Come back! You can't do that.

WARRIOR: Why?

ALEX: It's – just – not allowed.

WARRIOR: Ah. Another of your earth rules.

ALEX: Anyway, you don't need to bring Holly to me. Because – guess what? She asked me to her party today. Holly asked me! I think she must have liked my talk.

CAT: Oh dear. He's still in with a chance
  Of finding Holly-shaped romance!

WARRIOR: This party – is it a war party?

ALEX: No.

WARRIOR: A hunting party then?

ALEX: No! It's her birthday. She's having a snow party,
  outside, at the back of her house. See where all those
  fairy lights are? There's going to be food and music –

WARRIOR: Music!

ALEX: – and dancing. And Holly says she's having an
  enormous white cake in the shape of a snowman. And
  there'll be sledging and snowboarding and snowball
  fights –

WARRIOR: Fighting?

ALEX: Not real fighting. It's just for fun.

WARRIOR: Ah. Forfun. I remember forfun. It is when a
  person does the joking and the laughing. Hahaha. I like
  forfun. I shall come to this party.

ALEX: You can't. Sorry.

WARRIOR: Why not?

ALEX: You haven't been invited.

WARRIOR: But I have. The Agirl wants me to go and sing at
  her party.

ALEX: Holly asked you to go to her party?

WARRIOR: Me, you and your creature too. She thinks we
  are funny. Hahaha.

ALEX turns away from WARRIOR. CAT goes to ALEX.

CAT: Well, it seems the danger's passed.
Your firstluv chances didn't last.

Holly won't go with a bloke
If she sees him as a joke

ALEX: Funny…? She thinks I'm funny?

WARRIOR: Hahaha. Forfun.

ALEX does not respond.

I heard one of those – jokes – at skoolanstuff today.
Why are pirates called pirates? Because they 'aaarrrr'.
Hahaha.

ALEX does not respond.

Alex? What is troubling you, my friend?

ALEX: I'm not your friend! How can I be? You're not even
real!

WARRIOR: Not real?

ALEX: You don't come from a different world. You're out
of a stupid computer game! We're the real ones and we
made you up! You and your world are only pretend.

WARRIOR: Then – I am not made of stars?

ALEX: No! You're made of circuit boards and graphics cards
and pixels. You're not real! You're not real! You're not
real!

*Every repetition is a blow to WARRIOR. He staggers back. ALEX
runs off. CAT and WARRIOR share a look. CAT is torn between
sympathy for WARRIOR and following ALEX. WARRIOR makes
her choice for her. He exits the opposite side to ALEX. CAT looks
as though she is going to follow him but then turns back.*

SCENE THREE

CAT, SKARG 1, SKARG 2

CAT: (*Dithering.*) Should I let the Warrior go
Or make him stay? I just don't know!

If there are no Skarg in this place
We don't need him to keep us safe.

But without old leather-pants
Alex might still find romance.

Oh, this is such a quandary.
I can't decide what's best for me!

As CAT dithers, the space darkens and SKARG music begins to play. A Skarglike hissing begins. CAT hurries to the side of the space and flattens herself against the floor as the two SKARG appear, in insect form, carrying the sack of sugar they stole from the shop. They begin to cross the space but then stop as they catch CAT's scent. They cast around looking for her. CAT nips from hiding place to hiding place. The tension grows. At one point her tail is trapped in some way – perhaps under the sack. Finally, the SKARG exit.

SCENE FOUR

CAT, WARRIOR

CAT hurries back to the centre of the space and cries for help.

CAT: Warrior! Come back to me!
I need your help most urgently!

WARRIOR enters, sword at the ready. He checks the space.

WARRIOR: Why do you yowl so, creature? I thought you
and Alex must be in danger.

CAT: Oh, I've just seen such a sight!
I have to say that you were right.

The Skarg are back, in insect form
So please don't leave me here alone.

I really think you ought to stay.
I need protecting night and day.

WARRIOR: Where is your master, creature?

CAT: Oh, that's a point. He doesn't know
About the Skarg. Come on. Let's go.

WARRIOR: What's that you say, creature? He's fallen down
a mine shaft?

*CAT gives an eloquent shrug to the audience and goes into a
mime for WARRIOR's benefit in which she imitates a SKARG
threatening ALEX.*

(*After voicing several increasingly bizarre interpretations of
CAT's actions.*) Enough of your strange dancing! Alex is in
danger! Lead me to him!

CAT shrugs again and leads WARRIOR off.

SCENE 5

SKARG 1, SKARG 2

The SKARG enter in human form.

SKARG 1: The stolen sugar will keep our maggots happy for
now, Bananas, but we must find more.

SKARG 2: Yes, Nit, I know that. They must be fed with sugar
constantly until they start converting it into (*Makes a
hawking spitting sound.*).

SKARG 1: Excuse me. I think I was talking?

SKARG 2: Nit.

SKARG 1: Once the maggots can convert the sugar into
(*Hawk, spit.*) they will begin the change into fully grown

Skarg. Until then we must continue our ceaseless search for su... Su...urgh! What is that dreadful smell?

He looks at SKARG 2 *suspiciously.*

Bananas?

SKARG 2: It's not me, Nit!

SKARG 1: It smells like –

SKARG 1 / 2: Poo.

They both scan the audience suspiciously, sniffing.

SKARG 2: (*Pointing off.*) Zoo! Poo!

SKARG 1: Zoo poo?

SKARG 2: Correct, nit. Zoo poo. A zoo is a place where many different earth creatures live behind fences and humans pay to look at them. Where there is a zoo, there will be poo.

SKARG 1: Because of all the creatures. For instance, look at the size of that huge, grey beast. The one with the long, long nose and the enormous ears.

SKARG 2: An efelant.

SKARG 1: An efelant. A beast that size must make lots of –

Extended sound effect of an elephant having a poo. Both SKARG *react with horror and disgust. Just when they think it is over, the sound effects start up again. Finally –*

They will have to go.

SKARG 2: But look, Nit. The humans love the efelant. They are feeding it iced buns.

The SKARG *look at one another.*

BOTH: Sugar!

SKARG 2: Oh, Nit! We could disguise ourselves as zoo creatures and the humans will feed us iced buns. We could collect all the sugar we need for free!

SKARG 1: Not an efelant though. I absolutely refuse to do –

The elephant pooing sound effects start up again, lasting even longer than the first time. Again, the SKARG can hardly contain their disgust.

– that.

SKARG 2: Of course not. Besides, the humans would notice if two extra beasts of that size suddenly appeared. We must find a smaller creature. One that would not mind sharing its enclosure with us.

SKARG 1: And it must be – cute – to attract the humans. Access your data banks, Bananas.

SKARG 2 accesses her data banks and goes through a medley of songs/movie snippets with an animal theme, with SKARG 2 reacting to each new outburst accordingly. For example, 'In the jungle, the mighty jungle', 'Welcome to Jurassic Park', 'Nellie the efelant,' 'Crocodile rock,' 'Well I'm the king of the jungle' and so on. Finally she ends on a Pingu impression.

SKARG 2: Aha!

SKARG 1: Well? What form shall we take?

SKARG 2: Penguins. We shall become penguins.

The SKARG exit, turning into penguins as they go.

SCENE SIX

CAT, ALEX, WARRIOR, NEWSCASTER, TWO PENGUINS / SKARG

ALEX's bedroom. ALEX enters, thoroughly fed up. He slouches to the window and stares out. WARRIOR and CAT enter, running. CAT is completely out of breath.

WARRIOR: Alex!

ALEX turns, folds his arms, glares.

You are safe and well? But your Apet told me you were in danger. At least, I think that's what it said…

ALEX looks at WARRIOR as though he is mad. CAT finally recovers her breath enough to talk.

CAT: You are in danger, Alex dear
Old leather-pants was right, I fear.

The Skarg are here, as large as life
So please. You need him. Just be nice.

ALEX turns his back to WARRIOR and switches on his television. Through CAT's next speech, the NEWSCASTER comes into the screen/frame and settles down to read the news.

Don't listen then! I've had enough!
If you don't want to live, that's tough!

CAT plonks herself in front of the television. WARRIOR and ALEX stand facing one another. ALEX still angry, WARRIOR awkward.

NEWSCASTER: Winter. Icy mornings. Frozen pipes. Road chaos. But the snow isn't bad news for everyone.

Two penguins (SKARG in disguise) shuffle on stage.

WARRIOR: Television! I like the television.

ALEX does not respond.

NEWSCASTER: The penguins at the zoo are having a lovely time, as our reporter discovered earlier today when he asked them how they liked it there.

There follows a 'creature comforts'-type moment as the SKARG penguins talk to camera (with a 'North Pole' accent). Throughout this next scene, ALEX and WARRIOR are wordless, but what the PENGUINS *are saying obviously relates to their situation and they are responding to what is said.*

PENGUIN 1: Yes, ees nice here. Very nice. We ski.

PENGUIN 2: Ski.

PENGUIN 1: On zee ice slopes.

PENGUIN 2: Wheeee!

PENGUIN 1: We eat zee healthy fish... (*Tries to hide disgust.*) Yum.

PENGUIN 2: Fish...

PENGUIN 2 begins searching around. Eventually finds a fish under one flipper. Holds it up for the camera to see and narrowly misses slapping PENGUIN 1. CAT sits up at this and stares at the fish. PENGUIN 2 and CAT develop a routine. PENGUIN 2 moving the fish around and CAT following it.

PENGUIN 1: All very healthy. Very nice. Ees a good lifestyle. And people here, zey are very welcoming. Very – how you say – friendly. They feed us – with fish... (*Shudders.*) Yum.

PENGUIN 2 has had enough of CAT. It slides off-screen with the fish. PENGUIN 1 tries to ignore this.

We have come from far away. From a different land.

PENGUIN 2: (*Off.*) Far away...

PENGUIN 1: But we feel at home here. We have made many friends. We feel like we belong.

PENGUIN 1 looks offscreen, back to camera, then shuffles off after PENGUIN 2. Halfway off, he stops and points down at his flippers.

These will have to go!

NEWSCASTER: Aaah! What a heartwarming story. Hands across the world. Or should that be flippers? A lesson in friendship for us all.

NEWSCASTER pauses, looks for an 'ahh' response but is getting nothing. Sighs and continues.

Other news. A pair of sweet-toothed thieves broke into a local shop today – but all they stole was sugar.

Ashamed of his earlier outburst, ALEX is about to make things up with WARRIOR, but WARRIOR is suddenly transfixed by the news report. He is piecing things together.

ALEX: Warrior. About what I said earlier –

WARRIOR: Shhhh! Listen.

NEWSCASTER: The thieves were caught on CCTV cameras inside the shop but they were disguised. Inside giant insect costumes.

The SKARG appear in freeze-frame behind the NEWSCASTER. CAT screams and jumps away from the screen.

CAT / ALEX / WARRIOR: Skarg!

NEWSCASTER: Police are sending in a SWAT team.

Waits for laughter but CAT/ALEX/WARRIOR are staring at the SKARG freeze-frame in horror. NEWSCASTER imitates swatting a fly.

Fly – swat? SWAT team…? If that doesn't work, they're calling out the Flying Squad. *Fly*-ing squad? Oh, never mind. Good night – and thanks for listening.

NEWSCASTER gives up and shuffles off. SKARG remains in freeze-frame until WARRIOR/CAT/ALEX turn to look at one another, then they leg it off.

WARRIOR: Alex, this is much worse than I thought.

CAT: I know. His jokes are very poor
There really ought to be a law.

ALEX: How can it be worse? The Skarg are here and they're
out to get me!

CAT: (*To ALEX.*) That's what I've been telling you!
Is it finally getting through?

We need the Warrior to stay
And catch the Skarg and save the day.

I'm sure he'll manage just the two.
We'll leave him to it, me and you.

WARRIOR: (*Thinking aloud.*) I do not think they have come
through for revenge. There is only one reason for them
to collect sugar. They must have Skarg maggots to feed.

ALEX / CAT: Maggots?

WARRIOR: The Skarg are planning an invasion, Alex. This
is how it always starts. Two Skarg sneak in, rear an army
and then, only then, do they attack. We must find them
before the maggots change into Skarg.

ALEX: But how?

WARRIOR: They are still searching for maggot food. That is
a good sign. We are not too late. If we go where there is
sugar, we shall find the Skarg.

ALEX: Oh, no! Holly's snow party! There's a giant
snowman cake, with lots of sugar icing!

WARRIOR: Then let us go to this party!

ALEX, CAT and WARRIOR exit running.

SCENE SEVEN

ALEX, CAT, WARRIOR, SKARG 1 & 2 (DISGUISED AS PARTY
GUESTS), 'SNOWMAN CAKE', OTHER PARTY GUESTS (optional)

Party guests, including ALEX, CAT, WARRIOR and the two SKARG in human form, enter singing 'Frosty the Snowman' or similar. Some party guests hang icicles along the frame at the back of the space. A lantern should also be hung there. Others drape one of the party guests (this could be the actor playing the NEWSCASTER) in parachute silk, add a hat and scarf to transform him into a snowman cake. The SKARG are wary of being spotted at first but they want that cake for their maggots, so they stay. They begin to relax a bit as they realise the WARRIOR does not recognise them. The song comes to an end.

EVERYONE: Happy Birthday, Holly!

WARRIOR, CAT and ALEX go to stand beside the icicles. SKARG 1 and 2 try to edge the snowman cake off stage. They are also trying to avoid the WARRIOR and any other attention so their progress is slow. WARRIOR runs his hand across the icicles. They tinkle. The tinkling turns into soft snow music.

WARRIOR: What are these?

ALEX: Icicles.

WARRIOR: Are they a weapon?

ALEX: No.

WARRIOR: A defensive –

ALEX: No!

WARRIOR: Then they are not a kind of spear?

ALEX: No. They're frozen water.

WARRIOR runs his hand across them again. Listens to their music. Looks around.

WARRIOR: It is beautiful, this winter of yours.

ALEX: Yeah – and this is a great party.

WARRIOR: But we must leave now.

ALEX: We can't! I haven't had a chance to talk to Holly yet.

CAT: And the food is really nice
Salmon cakes and chocolate mice!

WARRIOR: The Skarg are not here. We must look elsewhere.

ALEX: But Holly wants you to sing now.

WARRIOR: Singing?

ALEX holds out a microphone.

Well, maybe just the one.

The rest of the party-goers become the chorus and dancers as WARRIOR launches into a schmaltzy version of 'Let it Snow, Let it Snow, Let it Snow' (or similar). The song finishes. The PARTY-GOERS applaud. As ALEX and CAT congratulate WARRIOR, SKARG 2 heads eagerly for the microphone. SKARG 1 attempts to stop her.

SKARG 1: Where are you going, Bananas?

SKARG 2: Listen to that applause! I'm gonna sing!

SKARG 1: You can't! We'll be spotted!

SKARG 2: Frankly, my dear, I don't give a damn.

SKARG 2 grabs the microphone, assumes a Marilyn Monroe pose beside the icicles and sings 'Diamonds Are a Girl's Best Friend' with backing from the other PARTY-GOERS. Another dance routine ensues. SKARG 1 edges the snowman cake to the side of the space. SKARG 2 sweeps her hat off and takes a bow. WARRIOR steps forward to shake her hand. He finally realises she is a SKARG.

WARRIOR: It's a Skarg!

SKARG 1 and 2 grab the snowman cake and hurry off.

WARRIOR / ALEX / CAT: After them!

SCENE EIGHT

SKARG 1, SKARG 2, ALEX, CAT, WARRIOR, SNOWMAN CAKE

The house lights come up as the actors use the whole space in a Keystone Cops style chase scene. Finally the SKARG both hide under the snowman cake's parachute silk and point off-stage. ALEX, CAT and WARRIOR rush off. The SKARG grab the snowman cake and head for the cave. The space darkens. The maggots begin to squeal in anticipation. The SKARG stuff the cake into the hole. There is the sound of ripping and chewing.

SKARG 2: Listen to them. Children of the night. What music they make.

SKARG 1: No thanks to you, Bananas. Penguins! Huh!

SKARG 2: I didn't know they only ate fish.

SKARG 1: Not my idea of a great time, being pelted with mouldy mackerel. What a stink!

Peering into the screen with his bottom sticking up in the air.

Oh, look at the little darlings! Is oo hungwy then? Is oo hungwy wungwy?

SKARG 2: Nit.

SKARG 1: (*Looking over his shoulder.*) Number twenty-three has the most adorable little black snout.

SKARG 2: They all have, Nit.

SKARG 1: And look at those chubby little segments – all pale and slimy! Oh, wait a minute.

SKARG 1 strikes a match/lights a candle and holds it over the maggot hole.

Yes! As I thought! It won't be long now. They've started converting the sugar into – into – what is the human name for (*Makes a noise as though he is hawking and spitting.*), Bananas?

SKARG 2 accesses her data banks.

SKARG 2: (*Hawk, spit.*) Aha! Rocket fuel.

SKARG 1 leans over the hole with the candle/match.

SKARG 1: Is oo making lots of rocket fuel for Daddy?

SKARG 2: Rocket fuel... Rocket fuel...

A look of horror crosses her face.

Houston we have a problem!

SKARG 1: What is it, Bananas?

SKARG 2: (*Backing off and pointing to the naked flame.*) In the atmosphere of this world, rocket fuel and fire together means – boom!

SKARG 1: Boom?

They both look at SKARG 1's match/candle. SKARG 1 quickly blows it out. They both back away from the screen.

SKARG 2: What do we do now, nit?

SKARG 1: You know, this parenting lark is very tiring. That cake will keep the maggots going for a while. I think we deserve some time off!

SKARG 2: Good idea, Nit! Let's go and see what this earth winter is all about.

SCENE NINE

SKARG 1, SKARG 2, ALEX, CAT, WARRIOR,
OTHER WINTER REVELLERS (optional)

'Walking in a Winter Wonderland' or similar begins to play as we see a montage of the SKARG 'time off'. They interfere with an animatronic window display, get caught up with a bobsled team on a luge run etc. At some point this becomes another chase scene as WARRIOR, CAT and ALEX recognise them. Suitable winter sports music plays as the whole company enacts a synchronised chase sequence using a whole range of activities such as snowboarding, skiing, ice-skating etc. The sequence comes to an end with everyone falling over. The SKARG make their escape.

SCENE TEN

ALEX, CAT, WARRIOR

ALEX, CAT and WARRIOR enter, out of breath.

CAT: Well, we're back at Holly's place.
Did we really have to chase

All over town? I feel quite weak.
I think I need something to eat.

Oh great, now that just makes my day!
The party food's been cleared away.

WARRIOR: Somewhere dark, Alex. If they have maggots, they'll need somewhere dark.

ALEX: But we've looked in every cellar, drain and underpass I can think of.

WARRIOR goes to lean against the frame. He notices the icicles have gone. Only the lantern remains.

WARRIOR: The frozen spears. They have melted away.

ALEX: That's odd. There's still snow everywhere else –

He looks up at Starwatcher's Hill.

– except on Starwatcher's hill! Look! It's all melted!

WARRIOR: The Skarg hatching process produces a lot of heat. They must be inside the hill, Alex!

ALEX: But how did they get in there? Wait a minute! There is a cave at the very top. I used to play in it when I was little. I'd forgotten all about it.

WARRIOR: Come on. We may yet be in time.

WARRIOR grabs the party lantern and follows ALEX off stage.

CAT: Why don't we just wait and see? Call the army out, maybe?

WARRIOR runs back onstage. He tries to explain to cat in sign language and miaows that they are going up Starwatcher's Hill. CAT stares. WARRIOR gives up. He throws CAT over his shoulder and exits after ALEX.

SCENE ELEVEN

SKARG 1, SKARG 2

The space becomes the cave. As SKARG 1 and 2 enter, an awful insectile screeching is heard.

SKARG 2: They are becoming Skarg!

SKARG 1: Then we must return to our true form and prepare to lead our army against the human settlement.

They both struggle to change as the insectlike screams grow in volume behind them. The struggle becomes more and more comical, but they remain human.

SKARG 2: Oh, Nit! Why can't we change into our Skarg form?

SKARG 1: We have become human, Bananas. We have grown to like this earth too much and now we are stuck in these bodies.

SKARG 2: Well this is another fine mess you've gotten me into!

SKARG 1: If they emerge and see us in our human form, what will happen to us?

SKARG 2: I see dead people...

SKARG 1: Perhaps if we take their sugar away we could stop them changing. Go and have a look Bananas.

SKARG 2 edges towards the frame – looks over – backs away.

SKARG 2: We're gonna need a bigger boat.

SKARG 1: A bigger what?

SKARG 2: They have already changed into fully grown Skarg. Soon they will begin climbing from the pit!

SKARG 1: Then perhaps they will still recognise us, even in our human form.

SKARG 1 edges to the screen and leans over with his bottom sticking in the air.

Hello my little baby wabies. It's your daddy-waddy – Oohh! Ouch! Yow! Gerrof!

SKARG 1 emerges looking worse for wear.

SKARG 2: Well?

SKARG 1: They just had their first taste of human – and I think they liked it.

SKARG 2: Oh, this is dreadful! Once they emerge, we shall become Skarg food or Skarg slaves, just like the rest of the human race! What can we do?

SKARG 1: There's only one thing left to do.

SKARG 1 / 2: Run!

SCENE TWELVE

ALEX, CAT, WARRIOR, SKARG 1, SKARG 2

The SKARG run from the maggots. WARRIOR, CAT and ALEX enter. The SKARG nearly run into WARRIOR with his sword drawn.

SKARG 1 / 2: Aaagggghhhh!

They run back to the cave. The maggots howl and hiss.

Aaaggghhh!

They run back to WARRIOR. He raises his sword

Aaagghhh!

Back to cave. The maggots howl.

Aaaggghh!

Back to WARRIOR.

SKARG 1: Evening.

SKARG 2: Nice night for a scream – I mean a stroll.

They begin to edge around WARRIOR but he stops them.

SKARG 1: Let us go! We have to get away!

WARRIOR: From what?

SKARG 2: Um… Nothing.

The SKARG scream sounds again.

SKARG 2: Except them…

ALEX: You were at the school pretending to be dentists!

SKARG 1: Us? No. You've got the wrong Skargs – I mean humans! We're humans.

ALEX: No you're not!

SKARG 2: (*Looking back at cave.*) We are now. Unfortunately.

WARRIOR: They speak the truth, Alex. They may have
been Skarg once, but now they are human.

The scream sounds again.

SKARG 1: Let us go! Please!

WARRIOR: Not until you tell me what is happening.

SKARG 1: All right! We'll tell you!

WARRIOR: I'm waiting.

SKARG 2: Oh, he's so masterful…

SKARG 1: Shut up, Bananas.

SKARG 2: (*To WARRIOR, as Marilyn.*)
I wanna be loved by you, just you and nobody else but
you,
I wanna be loved by you alone –

SKARG 1: I said, shut up!

ALEX: Are the maggots in the cave?

SKARG 1: There are no maggots in there… Because – they
have all become Skarg! Yes, Skarg! Soon they will
emerge from the cave and take over this puny planet!

ALEX: Oh, no! Holly's house is at the bottom of the hill!
She'll be one of the first ones killed! We have to stop
them.

SKARG 1: You cannot stop them. They are superb killing,
eating machines. They will destroy everything in their
path!

SKARG 2: Including us, Nit.

SKARG 1: Oh. Yes. I keep forgetting that.

CAT: Another species with no brains
I can't see much is going to change.

SKARG 2: And it is not only humans they will destroy. The Skarg army will wipe out every other species on the planet.

CAT: Even cats? (*To WARRIOR.*) Don't stand about! Go and sort the beggars out!

SKARG 1: There's nothing to be done now. They have all changed.

WARRIOR: There must be some way of stopping them.

SKARG 2: There is one chance. When the maggots feed on the sugar, they produce something known on this planet as rocket fuel.

WARRIOR: Yes?

SKARG 2: If a flame is dropped into the rocket fuel, it will explode – Boom!

SKARG 1: Now just a minute –

SKARG 2: And the hatchlings are still at the bottom of the hole. In the rocket fuel.

WARRIOR looks at the lantern he is holding. He nods in understanding.

SKARG 1: Bananas! I order you to stop now!

SKARG 2: Shut up, Nit! I'm talking to a real man!

SKARG 1: Oh! How dare you! I'll have you court-martialled!

SKARG 2: Toto, we're not in Kansas any more.

SKARG 1: Excuse me?

SKARG 2: We're stuck on earth now. You can't tell me what to do any more. Nit.

SKARG 1: Mutiny!

SKARG 2: No. Survival. Do you really want those Skarg to come out of that pit? Think about it. Phone a friend. Ask the audience.

SKARG 1 splutters. The hatchlings scream. He turns to WARRIOR and points at the lantern

SKARG 1: Hurry up! They won't stay down there for long!

SKARG 2: Can I go now?

CAT: You can't let those two wander free! They'll head off on a trouble spree!

SKARG 2: Please...

WARRIOR: What do you think, Alex?

ALEX: I don't know. What if they try to bring more Skarg through to this world?

SKARG 2: Why would we do that? We are human now.

WARRIOR: If I let you leave, do you promise not to cause trouble in this world?

SKARG 1: Promise? You ask a Skarg to bow to a human? How dare you!

SKARG 2 kicks SKARG 1.

Ow!

SKARG 2: I promise.

ALEX: What will you do?

SKARG 2: I'm gonna go to Hollywood. I'm gonna be a star!

WARRIOR: A star?

ALEX: Not that sort of star. She's going to find work in Tinsel-town.

CAT: Here's a line to memorise
'Would you like ketchup on those fries?'

WARRIOR: Very well. You can go.

SKARG 2 heads off eagerly.

But you must take him with you.

SKARG 2: I want to be alone.

WARRIOR: No. He needs watching.

SKARG 2: You don't understand! I coulda had class. I coulda been a contender.

WARRIOR: Take him with you, or stay here. That's the deal.

SKARG 2 glares at SKARG 1 who attempts an ingratiating smile. SKARG 2 begins to leave, with SKARG 1 following. She stops, turns back.

SKARG 2: (*To WARRIOR.*) May the force be with you.

The SKARG make their escape. WARRIOR goes up to the screen and peers over.

ALEX: Go on then, Warrior. Throw the lantern in. Then we'll run down the hill as fast as we can!

WARRIOR looks back at ALEX.

WARRIOR: I cannot do that Alex.

ALEX: It's easy! Just let the lantern drop!

WARRIOR: And what if it hits a ledge on the way down?

ALEX: Warrior…?

The scream comes again.

WARRIOR: One chance, Alex. That's all we have.

ALEX: Warrior!

WARRIOR: Stand back, Alex.

ALEX: Don't jump!

WARRIOR: I have to, Alex. I cannot watch this earth of yours become the same as my own planet.

ALEX: But there's no New Game in this world.

WARRIOR: I had not forgotten.

ALEX: If you jump, you won't return!

WARRIOR: But I will save the world! Isn't that what a hero is for, Alex?

ALEX is silent. WARRIOR turns, prepares to jump.

ALEX: Warrior? I didn't mean it when I said you weren't real. I never stopped believing in you.

WARRIOR: I know that.

ALEX: How?

WARRIOR: Because I never stopped believing in you.

WARRIOR holds out his hand. ALEX grips it. WARRIOR looks at CAT. CAT honours him with a courtly bow. WARRIOR nods at CAT. He climbs up onto the blocks and jumps. There is a huge rumbling explosion and a flash of orange light. ALEX and CAT manoeuvre the blocks in slow motion, creating the effect of debris flying through the air.

SCENE THIRTEEN

ALEX, CAT, WARRIOR, STAR

ALEX: Warrior? Warrior?

CAT: Be careful, Alex, watch your step
There might just be a few Skarg left.

ALEX: There's no cave any more. Just a big crater.

CAT: Is there nothing left alive?
Old leather-pants? Did he survive?

ALEX: The rocket fuel blasted everything up into the sky.
He's gone. He's really gone.

CAT: How strange. Why would he jump right in
Instead of saving his own skin?

Is this what you call 'sacrifice'?
We cats would never pay that price.

ALEX: Oh, Snowball! I told him he didn't belong here.
I told him he wasn't made of stars. I wish I hadn't
done that.

CAT: We all say mean things when we're mad.
He understood that. Don't be sad.

ALEX: He was a hero, Snowball. He saved us all. I told him
he wasn't real, but he was.

CAT: Shhh! Please don't get so upset.
You've still got me. I'll be your pet.

ALEX: So what if he wasn't made of stars? It's what you do
that makes you real, not what you're made of. Oh…

ALEX gasps and points.

Look Snowball…

*CAT looks up. They both stare. WARRIOR reappears, transformed
into a star / constellation in the sky. They smile.*

SCENE FOURTEEN

ALEX, CAT, WARRIOR (as Winter Star)
NEWSCASTER, HOLLY, OTHER STARWATCHERS

NEWSCASTER enters as news bulletin music plays.

NEWSCASTER: Here is the news!

Police and Scientists are still investigating the cause of a huge explosion, when the top of a hill known locally as Starwatcher's Hill was blown into the sky.

Other STARWATCHERS enter (including SKARG actors wearing woolly hats etc.)

Speaking of strange events, a computer game company has issued a product recall notice after the game's main character, known as The Warrior, disappeared from screens all over the world.

And finally, a local boy has discovered a new Winter Star.

WARRIOR, as Winter Star, becomes centre of attention. ALEX looks up at him and smiles.

It is the custom for the person who discovers a star to name it after themselves, but Alex has broken with this tradition, choosing to name this star The Warrior. When asked, Alex would not explain his decision but Holly, a fellow starwatcher, told us that Alex has named the star in memory of a friend.

Astronomers have already picked up a pulse of sound from this new star. They say it sounds like nothing they have ever heard before.

WARRIOR sings his favourite song, 'Let it Snow' or similar, sotto vocce. He continues through the rest of NEWSCASTER's bulletin.

So, next time you step out into the dark, look up. You will be amazed!

Goodnight – and thanks for listening.

ALEX, CAT and the other starwatchers sing the last verse of 'Twinkle twinkle little star'. Star music plays.

The End.